Horse

For Sandra and Tim
MD

For Olivia
Thanks to Kimberly Berry, Deen City Farm
and Deanhills Stud for all their help
AR

SIMON AND SCHUSTER

First published in Great Britain in 2008 by Simon & Schuster UK Ltd
Africa House, 64-78 Kingsway, London WC2B 6AH
A CBS COMPANY

Text copyright © 2008 Malachy Doyle
Illustrations copyright © 2008 Angelo Rinaldi
The right of Malachy Doyle and Angelo Rinaldi to be identified as the author
and illustrator of this work has been asserted by them in accordance
with the Copyright, Designs and Patents Act, 1988

Book designed by Genevieve Webster

A CIP catalogue record for this book is available from
the British Library upon request

ISBN 978 0 6898 3503 2 (HB)
ISBN 978 1 4169 1103 6 (PB)

Printed in China
1 3 5 7 9 10 8 6 4 2

Horse

Malachy Doyle

Angelo Rinaldi

SIMON AND SCHUSTER
London • New York • Sydney

A horse stands alone in a field.
She is waiting.

The children come to visit her.
They love her warm, sweet smell,
and the way her breath comes
hot and heavy from her soft nose.

They stroke her velvety muzzle,
talking quietly to her.
And the horse waits, still.

On a soft spring night,
the foal is born.
Slowly, his mother rises to
her feet and licks him all over.

By dawn he is up on his long spindly legs,
peeping out at the children
who come to welcome him into the world.

The colt grows quickly, greeting each new day
by thudding his hooves on the damp earth,
shaking his stubby tail and rushing
around the field.

But as the summer sun rises to its height,
the young colt's ears droop forward,
his legs fold under him and he dozes,
stretched out on the grass, with his mother
watching over him.

As the leaves begin to fall and the light begins to fade,
the big old mare droops her neck for the bridle once more.
Soon she is trotting round the field,
with her foal racing to keep up.

By winter, his coat is thick and sleek.
The colt grows bigger and stronger every day,
kicking up the snow with his hooves
as he charges round the paddock.

Then, one fine spring morning,
the girl offers him a carrot.
As the yearling leans forward,
she slips a rope around his neck
and puts a head collar over his warm,
silken nose.

Stroking his head, talking softly,
she leads him quietly round the field.
"You're such a beautiful horse," she tells him.

"One day we're going to ride, you and I,
over the hill and all the way to the sea…"

Praise for COW by Malachy Doyle and Angelo Rinaldi:

*The cows are so close up you can almost hear the snorting breath;
feel the mud and dew. It is a reality shot through with luminous magic.*

The Independent

*The nearest thing to meeting a real cow in a field
that children could ever get within the pages of a book.*

The Observer

*A perfect evocation of the cowness of a cow. Sumptuously illustrated
by Angelo Rinaldi with gorgeously detailed oil paintings.*

Independent on Sunday